ALL ABOUT GRIEF

by
Dr. Lora-Ellen McKinney

illustrated by
Sophia Touliatou

beaming books
MINNEAPOLIS

29 28 27 26 25 24   2 3 4 5 6 7 8 9

Hardcover ISBN: 978-1-5064-9127-1
eBook ISBN: 978-1-5064-9128-8

Library of Congress Cataloging-in-Publication Data

Names: McKinney, Lora-Ellen., author.
Title: All about grief / by Dr. Lora-Ellen McKinney ; illustrated by Sophia
    Touliatou.
Description: Minneapolis, MN : Beaming Books, 2024. | Audience: Ages 9-13 |
    Summary: "All About Grief looks at grief from many different angles,
    helping preteens understand how it influences emotions, relationships,
    brains, bodies, and behavior"-- Provided by publisher.
Identifiers: LCCN 2023019493 (print) | LCCN 2023019494 (ebook) | ISBN
    9781506491271 (hardback) | ISBN 9781506491288 (ebook)
Subjects: LCSH: Grief--Juvenile literature. | Emotions--Juvenile
    literature.
Classification: LCC BF575.G7 M428 2024 (print) | LCC BF575.G7 (ebook) |
    DDC 155.9/37--dc23/eng/20230802
LC record available at https://lccn.loc.gov/2023019493
LC ebook record available at https://lccn.loc.gov/2023019494

Beaming Books
PO Box 1209
Minneapolis, MN 55440-1209
Beamingbooks.com

TABLE OF CONTENTS

CHAPTER 1
WHAT IS GRIEF?

Hello, grief.
Let's get to know
each other!

Have you ever moved away from your friends? It might have felt like a deep sadness that made you cry or feel angry, helpless, or overwhelmed. Why? Because you'll miss walking to school with them, sharing jokes, hanging out. Or your pet ran away and hasn't returned, and you understand that you won't get to play with them anymore. Or maybe someone you know has died, and you're sad that you will never see them again. The emotion that you probably felt is called grief. You loved your friends, your pet, or that person so much that losing them hurts. It hurts your brain, your body, and your spirit.

I like to define grief as deep sadness or sorrow.

That's right! Grief happens when we lose something or someone very important to us.

Grief is a normal, natural response to loss.
Everyone experiences grief. You can't avoid it.
Grief can be hard to understand and talk about.

Everyone experiences grief in different ways. Grief can take your breath away. Sometimes grief feels like somebody punched you in the stomach so hard that tears got pushed out of your eyes and down your face. Sometimes you just feel bad in a way that is hard to explain.

This book looks at grief from many different angles, examining how grief influences our emotions and relationships, our brains and bodies, and our behavior. You'll get to know when and why we are most likely to grieve, what purpose grief serves, and strategies for healing. Some strategies can be explored on your own, while others will require assistance from an adult you love or trust, or from an expert in helping people heal from grief. Read on and see if any examples from your life are in these pages.

Top Tip!

Your grief may feel like this math equation. It feels complicated, but it becomes easier to understand and manage when we break it down.

Loss + Sorrow (Deep Sadness) + Emotional Pain + Anger + Confusion = Grief

HOW DO YOU TALK ABOUT GRIEF?

Everyone experiences grief. Since grief is a common emotion, why don't people talk about it more? Most people prefer to talk about happy things. Grief is not a happy topic of conversation, but it is very important to discuss. One reason so many people avoid talking about grief is that they don't have the right words to discuss sad feelings. Look at this list of words that are synonyms for sadness. How many have you heard used in conversations?

- bad (feeling wounded and unwell)
- blue (sad or depressed)
- brokenhearted (overwhelmed by grief and disappointment)
- depressed (saddened and unhappy)
- despairing (having no hope)
- despondent (low spirits from the loss of love)
- heartsick (sadness from grief or loss of love)
- melancholy (a thoughtful sadness)
- mournful (experiencing sadness, regret, or grief)

These words are all useful for explaining grief, yet each is slightly different. It's no wonder even adults find it hard to talk about grief. If the adults in your life experienced the same loss of a parent or friend or pet that you did, they are probably grieving too. They may not find it easy to understand their own feelings. For that reason, and because the language for discussing sad feelings can seem complicated, even these adults who know you best may find it hard to help you sort out your feelings or understand the full impact of your grief.

Many people think having conversations about grief will make everyone feel worse. That is not usually true. Conversations about grief are definitely not easy, but when we talk about our grief, it can help us get better.

"Some people say that 'Grief is love with nowhere to go.' What does this quote mean to you?"

I think it means that when the person or pet you loved is dead, you can't love them anymore.

Actually, you don't stop loving someone or something when they die. But for a period of time, grief makes your sadness and feelings of love get stuck inside you. Or it may make you feel unable to function normally.

GRIEF NAVIGATORS

Imagine your life as a road that takes you from childhood to adulthood. You develop different skills as you get older, and people in your life—family members, teachers, social workers, faith leaders, therapists, and medical doctors—serve as navigators. A navigator is someone who helps you get from place to place, a bit like a human GPS.

Because grief is a complicated issue, this book provides you with several kinds of Grief Navigators. Like the trusted people in your life, they will help you better understand grief. As you meet each of these characters, think about who might fill similar roles in your own life. It's OK if you can't think of someone for every category of navigator. Or maybe one person fills multiple roles! Having real life Grief Navigators in a few of these areas is an important tool when understanding and healing from grief.

- **The Friends** are kids just like you who have questions about grief.
- **Adults Who Care** are trusted people you know—parents, teachers, coaches, neighbors—who are available to support you when you grieve, even if they are grieving themselves.
- **The Faith Council** is a group of spiritual leaders whose understanding of grief and tips on managing emotional pain may be related to their religious beliefs.
- **The Science Council** is made up of different kinds of doctors and scientists who study causes of grief and its impact on children's brains, bodies, and emotions. This group has scientists who study biology, climate, the human body, and the mind.
- **Counselor Kamala** is a child psychologist who is specially trained to help children understand their feelings. It is good for kids to have a trusted adult to talk to who is not their parent. Therapy (also called counseling) is a safe space for kids to talk about their grief and heal from the pain it causes.

PICTURE GRIEF

When we experience a loss, grief moves into our bodies and our brains. It can leave us feeling numb and overwhelmed. Visualizing grief can help us manage these feelings.

An uninvited guest

Has someone ever shown up at your house without an invitation? Then, when you open the door, they walk right in? Grief is like that. Grief is an unexpected and uninvited guest that walks right into your life. As with the case of the uninvited houseguest, you try everything you can to get them to leave. Grief can be stubborn: it may hang out inside you for longer than you'd like. Remember to check in with your Grief Navigators, exercise, eat well, and do some of the self-care activities found throughout this book. Healing is a decision: just like with an uninvited guest, you decide when to show grief to the door and ask it to leave.

Tilly Tumbleweed

Tilly Tumbleweed is a prickly plant whose size changes as grief gets worse or better. A tumbleweed is a thistle, a plant skeleton that is found in the American desert. It breaks off from its base when it dies, drying into a round tangle of poky branches. Tumbleweeds can start out small, but as the wind blows them across the desert, they pick up twigs and plants, growing larger and larger and larger.

Did you know that tumbleweeds are also called wind witches? They are symbols of sadness, unknown destinations, and emptiness. In addition to picking up trash, they soak up contamination from the soil. Like a tumbleweed, grief can make you soak up sadness and other negative feelings, and feel stuck in emotions you do not understand. If you don't talk to someone you trust about your grief, it can grow and have unexpected impacts on your physical and emotional health.

Your grief may shrink or grow, just like a tumbleweed. Sometimes your grief will be a small tumbleweed. It won't travel far or gather many twigs and spiny parts that poke and prod you. Other times, your grief tumbleweed will get larger, travel far down the road, and be a challenge for you to manage. Sometimes you might have different kinds of tumbleweeds that find each other and become a huge ball of grief.

Brickmason BOW

Brickmason BOW is a builder whose wall gets bigger when you are sad and smaller when you begin to heal. Brickmasons build walls and buildings by stacking bricks in rows, one on top of the other, to create a barrier. Walls are barriers that protect the people behind them and keep strangers from entering or looking in.

When you first experience grief, a wall can help you feel safe. But to heal from grief, you need to keep your emotional bricks from piling up too high. If your grief has already built a tall wall, you can learn to take the wall down safely, one brick at a time. We'll explore ways to do so later.

Healing from grief involves BRICK or WALL (BOW) choices:

- **WALL OPTION** – You are in pain from losing someone or something important to you. You can build a wall of as many bricks as you need to protect yourself. Your grief tumbleweed will be out of sight behind the wall.

- **BRICK OPTION 1** – Remove bricks from your wall to let in people who can help you understand your feelings. When you talk about your grief and label your feelings, you feel safer and less overwhelmed.

- **BRICK OPTION 2** – You remove bricks from your wall as you use the tools you have learned from your Grief Navigators. As the bricks are removed from your wall, your grief tumbleweed shrinks and shrivels, and you begin to feel better.

DIFFERENT TYPES OF GRIEF

These are the most common types of grief that have been identified by experts. You might recognize them after reading the descriptions. You may have noticed them in people you know. You may have experienced some of them too. Everyone will experience one or more of these forms of grief during their life.

Normal grief

Any time you suffer the loss of a person, pet, or source of safety, it is very normal to have feelings of grief. Grief can show up in your body, behavior, feelings, and relationships. By practicing self-care strategies at home, you can lessen this type of grief over time.

Chronic grief

Chronic grief is extreme feelings of loss that do not go away and remain very painful after four to six weeks. Because it does not seem to go away, it can cause a lot of worry and grow into a large tumbleweed. Chronic grief is very hard to heal without the help of a trained professional.

Cumulative grief

When you experience a new form of grief before you have healed from an earlier grieving experience, you might experience cumulative grief. If you experience different kinds of loss in a short amount of time, it is possible to experience more than one kind of grief at the same time. Your grief may also change to a different type, sometimes one that is harder to heal.

Cumulative grief can also be called grief overload. Based on the definition of cumulative grief, it is easy to see how anyone who has had grief pile up on them would feel overloaded or overwhelmed, but any form of grief can create emotional overload or be overwhelming.

Overwhelming feelings of loss and sadness are normal responses to grief. Everyone processes grief differently. Some people find that stress and anxiety keep them from healing from their grief. If you're feeling overloaded or overwhelmed, talk to someone. With a listening ear and guidance from the right caring adults, therapist, or counselor, it is possible to manage your feelings and heal from your grief.

Delayed grief

Sometimes your grief starts a long time after you experience a loss. Delayed grief happens when the loss is too painful for you to feel right away. Your mind builds a wall to protect you from the immediate experience of emotional pain, blocking you from feeling emotions that are usually part of the grief process.

Exaggerated grief

Exaggerated grief happens when normal grief responses intensify. This involves reactions to grief that are more extreme than in the other types of grief. The bad feelings can get more extreme over time. You might experience abnormal fears, nightmares, or other mental-health issues that require treatment with therapy and/or medication.

Distorted grief

Distorted grief is an extreme reaction to a loss. Grief hits us hard. When there is a lot of emotional pain from grief, our emotions can get distorted. Distortions warp and twist our feelings in ways that go beyond normal grief, causing changes to our personality. Behavior may change in a way that is disruptive, is hard for other people to ignore, and may involve actions that are dangerous to other people or to the grieving person themself.

If you experience these signs of distorted grief, you'll need professional help to feel better.

Masked grief

You might wear masks for parties or as part of a fun costume. They cover parts of your face and keep other people from seeing you clearly. Grief sometimes hides behind a mask. Masked grief often shows up as physical symptoms and behaviors that interfere with your daily activities. You notice that you don't feel well or are not really acting like yourself, but you don't know why. The emotional mask lets you hide your pain, but it keeps you—and others—from seeing the truth. Masked grief can look like nightmares, lashing out at others, and thoughts of self-harm.

Collective grief

Collective grief happens when a whole community or large group of people grieves the same event. This form of grief is common when the event is very public and affects many people. Grieving may be intense even when death is not involved, such as the loss of a home or a change in your sense of security.

On the news

Our grief can be caused or affected by what we see on television. For example, George Floyd was a Black man who was murdered by a police officer in Minneapolis, Minnesota, in 2020. His death was widely shown on television and the internet because a young girl named Darnella Frazier recorded it on her phone. This murder horrified people all around the world. They marched in the streets, saying "Black Lives Matter!"

Tyre Nichols was a young Black man murdered by five police officers in Memphis, Tennessee, in 2023. This was a devastating, video-recorded, and widely publicized death as well. In these cases, and for many others, communities grieved deeply because the events were shocking and cruel. They made people feel unsafe. They made children, especially children of color, wonder if they could trust police officers whose job was to protect them. This contributed to the confusion that often accompanies grief.

In widely publicized cases like these, victims' families are often asked to make statements just days after the death. They are not given the time they may require to grieve personally because government officials, civil rights leaders, and others feel the need to hear from them. It is important to remember that while grief can be collective, it is also a highly personal process. All people, families, and communities should be allowed to determine their own way to grieve without being pushed beyond a place of comfort or into a public role, unless they want it.

Traumatic grief

Traumatic grief is the result of trying to understand and heal from a sudden, unexpected, violent, or accidental death of someone to whom a person is closely attached (parent, grandparent, sibling, beloved friend, etc.). Traumatic grief can interfere with daily functioning in similar ways as other kinds of grief, but the emotions related to traumatic grief are usually much more intense. Traumatic grief is more likely to lead to more complicated behaviors and symptoms, as well as other forms of grief. For example, people experiencing traumatic grief may experience disturbed dreams, post-traumatic stress disorder (PTSD), or difficulty being happy.

WHO GRIEVES?

Everybody!

So how will you know when your grief has stopped being a normal response to loss and has turned into a problem? Maybe your grief tumbleweed feels too prickly and big and complicated to manage on your own, or your brick wall is too tall to see over or too hard to knock down.

It's possible that you won't understand what you are feeling. A friend may notice that you are not your normal self. In these cases, you should find one of your Grief Navigators (a school counselor or therapist, a caregiver, a faith leader) and talk to them about it. They are there to support you and help you feel better.

Here are some ways to think about healing from grief:

- Healing takes time.

- Healing means that you are capable of deeply loving someone or something.

- Healing requires help from other people. It is hard to do alone.

- Healing is an important decision. You decide that it is time to feel better.

- Healing from grief is a new way of thinking about the loss you've experienced.

CHAPTER 2
WHAT CAUSES GRIEF?

where exactly does grief come from?

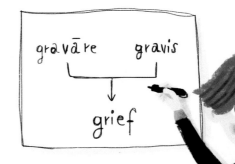

The word *grief* was first used in the year 1200. It comes from the Latin verb *gravre*, which means "to burden," and the adjective *gravis*, which means "heavy." Do these Latin words sound familiar? Both *grave* (which means "serious") and *gravity* ("heaviness in time and space") share the same root word!

Understanding the word *grief* helps us understand how it makes us feel. Grief has weight. Grief is a heavy and weighty emotion.

—**Social Scientist Sara**, a sociologist who studies the ways we act in groups and how grief becomes a shared experience in community

Grief comes from painful changes to our everyday lives, and different kinds of loss lead to different kinds of pain. The type of loss and the experience of grief will vary from one person to another.

Death of a loved one

This loss can be the death of a family member, a good friend, or a family pet.

Loss of something important and irreplaceable

Now, if you lose a quarter because there is a hole in your coat pocket, that kind of loss makes you annoyed, but it won't cause you to grieve. But maybe you misplaced the bracelet your friend made you before moving away. That was an important gift and was special to you, so it's understandable that losing it would make you feel really sad.

Ending of an important relationship

This loss can occur from big changes, like when parents get divorced, when you move into foster care, or when your family moves far away from your friends. Or grief can be the response to the breakup of a relationship or friendship, whether these events occurred abruptly or resulted from growing apart.

Moving away

Your parents might have decided to move to a new home, or you need to leave because of a natural disaster or an eviction. Moving to a new place can cause grief, as it can create a lot of uncertainty for you. It may mean saying goodbye to your friends and places where you have made memories. Your home is the place that you connect with comfort, safety, and special memories. Moving away from that place and those feelings can cause you to grieve. You may feel sad about what you are leaving behind, and you don't know what and who you will encounter in your new home.

Injury or loss of good health

Whether temporary or permanent, changes to your body can affect your mental health. Imagine that you broke your leg at summer camp. You might feel grief over a loss of independence, since you now need help from others to get around. Or maybe you planned to join your school's basketball team. Because your leg needs to heal, you can't play basketball. You might feel grief that your dream is gone.

Illnesses or medical experiences can shock and surprise us. These unexpected challenges can be confusing and sometimes change how we view ourselves in ways that make us very sad.

COVID-19

In December 2019, a new virus started making people sick all around the world with a disease called COVID-19. To stay safe, families had to stay in their homes while scientists learned how the disease spread. It caused a lot of fear because no one knew what to do. People also grieved a loss of normalcy, as they couldn't go to school or work or attend events like weddings or funerals. By the summer of 2022, over 250,000 children had a parent or caregiver who had died from COVID-19. Over half of these kids were Black or Latinx and were more likely to get sick or die than white Americans because of poverty, crowded housing conditions, dangerous work conditions, and racial violence that impacted larger numbers of those groups.

The COVID-19 pandemic shows us how different forms of grief can build on top of each other, and how people can be impacted by the same event in very different ways.

Loss of safety

Sometimes, scary events happen in places we go, like when a shooting happens at a school. You might have experienced something like this yourself or heard about such things on the news. As a result, you might not feel safe returning to school. Or you may have safety drills at school to prepare for something scary happening. Just having to participate in these exercises can cause fear, anxiety, and grief. It is OK to experience feelings of grief while processing the event and the changes to your life.

You might feel unsafe because of bullying, which is when someone tries to harm, embarrass, humiliate, or deliberately hurt someone else. Getting bullied is frightening and traumatic. It can cause grief because we might lose friends, sleep, and self-esteem. If you or someone you know is being bullied, please tell a trusted adult.

Climate

In 2021, researchers at the University of Bath in the United Kingdom spoke to 10,000 young people in ten countries about climate change. The researchers found that young people are concerned about protecting the climate as a way to honor the earth and secure their futures. Many young people say climate change makes them feel sad, afraid, anxious, angry, and powerless. Young people have also been frustrated because governments are moving too slowly to pass laws and regulations that can save the planet.

—**Roc the Earth Science Doc**, an expert in what the earth is made of, how it works, and what has changed over time

Adults in your life are experiencing grief

Some things that happen to adults can have an impact on you, especially if you live with them. If a parent or guardian loses a job, it can make the family unstable, and you might grieve the loss of stability, regular meals, nice clothing, or a familiar home. Maybe a guardian retired from working at their job. They may grieve that change, which could interrupt the family's routines and feelings of safety. Or someone close to you may become ill, which can cause grief because it means that health, patterns of behavior, and spending time with that person are at risk.

IS THERE A BIOLOGICAL REASON FOR GRIEF?

Evolutionary biology, the study of how life has changed throughout history, provides one theory about how our minds and bodies developed to process grief. Evolutionary biologists think grief has an important role in evolution.

Think of your brain as a video game. There are rewards for scoring points, and missing targets leads to losses. Our brains have reward centers. These centers create happy brain chemicals when we have fun alone or with a group of people. But losing an opportunity or missing someone can make us feel sad. According to these scientists, when human beings lived in forests among big and dangerous animals, grief was an emotion that was essential for our survival. By missing "targets," the brain's lack of happy brain chemicals lasted long enough for us to search for a loved one who might be lost. Grief would eventually fade away when we understood that we could not find our lost loved one because they had died, moved far away, or no longer wanted to be our friend.

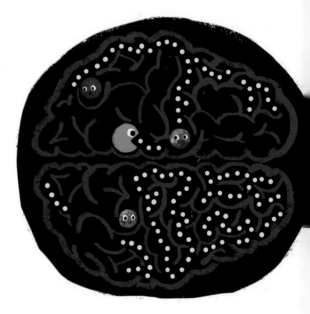

CHAPTER 3
HOW DOES GRIEF SHOW UP IN YOUR BODY AND BRAIN?

Grief is an experience that is physical and psychological. That means that when we lose someone or something we love, grief changes the ways our bodies function and our minds work.

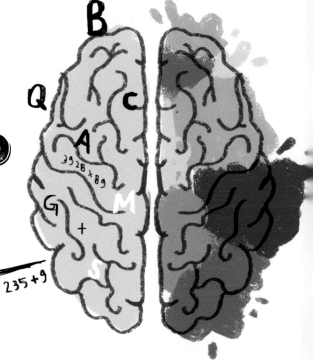

YOUR GRIEVING BRAIN

The brain is a three-pound organ in our heads that is made up of nerve cells. It is our command center, in charge of what we do, think, and feel. The brain is divided into two halves, a right and a left hemisphere. The two halves look very similar but work in different ways and serve different functions. The left brain hemisphere handles reading, writing, and arithmetic. It uses logic to process information from our immediate senses (taste, hearing, touch, smell, sight). The right brain hemisphere uses more images than words. It processes visual shapes and our emotions. It expresses itself through nonverbal activity (body language, tone of voice, eye movements).

Human brains are EACH/AND organs. Each hemisphere of the brain addresses and processes things in its own way (EACH) *and* as a coordinated set with the other hemisphere (AND). For example, we usually think of language as coming from the left hemisphere. But it is the right hemisphere that interprets the tone of the language that is spoken or heard. Imagine a choir. There are sopranos, altos, tenors, and basses, all singing the same song. But each has a different note; their *tones* are different. Different people can speak the same sentence, but they will have different tones. The two sides of our brains work together to understand the verbal communication (left hemisphere) and nonverbal meaning (right hemisphere) in our words.

Going to therapy when you are grieving is important. A trained professional can evaluate if your emotion matches your words, tone, and body language.

Healing from grief is a balance: words = tone = body language

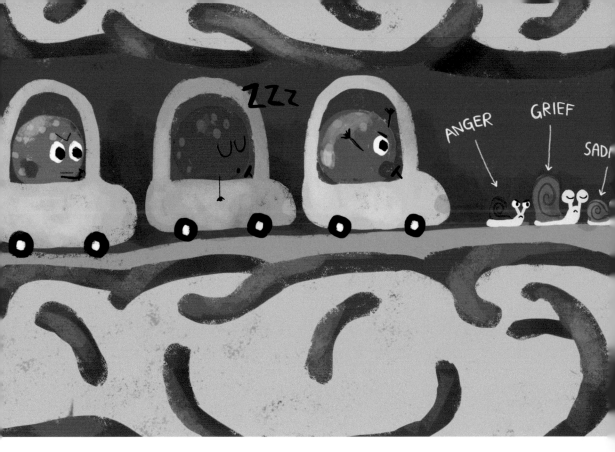

Between the hemispheres is a nerve bridge, called the corpus callosum. This nerve bridge is your brain's information superhighway. It ensures that the two sides of the brain send signals to each other. They communicate back and forth, almost like two players in a tennis game. But when grief occurs, traffic jams and accidents confuse the brain's normal communication patterns.

When you grieve, your brain can get overloaded with sadness, loneliness, anxiety, and anger. We call this Grief Brain. Grief Brain makes it harder to remember, concentrate, and learn.

DOES GRIEF CHANGE THE CHEMICALS IN THE BRAIN?

Brains have important chemicals—called neurotransmitters and hormones—that carry information between the cells in your brain and to the rest of your body. When you grieve, the chemicals in your brain and body can change, influencing your mood and health. Neurotransmitters like serotonin and dopamine are directly linked to our emotions; low levels of these might cause anxiety or depression. Hormones like the corticotrophin-releasing factor (CRF) control our stress. When we grieve, our brains produce more CRF, which can negatively affect our sleep, appetite, memory, and attention.

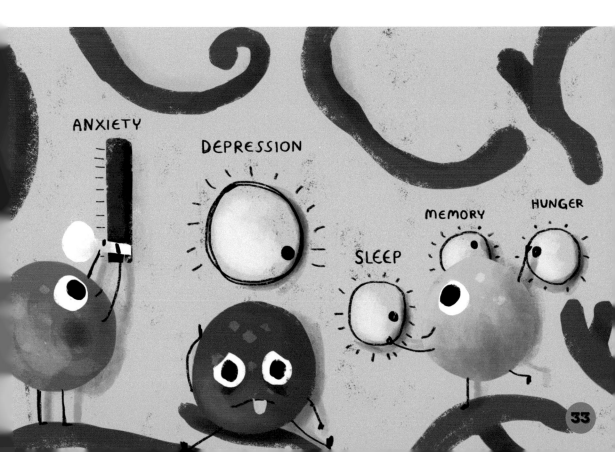

ANXIETY

DEPRESSION

MEMORY

HUNGER

SLEEP

Because grief affects the chemicals in our brains, it can trigger different kinds of feelings:

- anger
- anxiety
- depression
- guilt
- lack of motivation
- loneliness
- the wish to run away and hide

When you grieve, brain chemicals dance around in your brain. Their dance is not a pretty ballet or a waltz. The chemical grief dance is more a freestyle set of jumps, stops, spins, thumps, and starts. This dance leaves little room for regular, everyday tasks and activities.

—**Neurologist Abeba**, a scientist who knows all about the brain, spinal cord, and nervous system

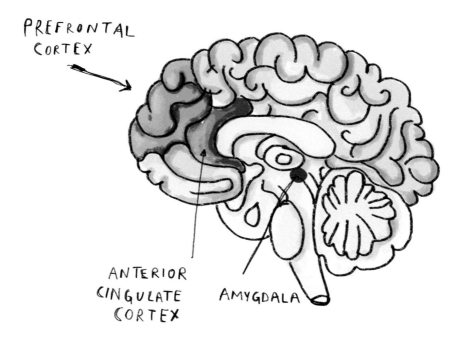

PREFRONTAL
CORTEX

ANTERIOR
CINGULATE
CORTEX

AMYGDALA

Your brain has different regions that process grief and are affected by these chemicals.

THE PREFRONTAL CORTEX, the "thinking center" of the brain, has trouble concentrating, thinking clearly, and learning.

THE ANTERIOR CINGULATE CORTEX, the "emotions center" of the brain, has trouble regulating feelings, resulting in anxiety and anger.

THE AMYGDALA, the "fear center" of the brain, has trouble processing strong emotions and interpreting threats and danger (activating our fight-or-flight response more often).

Grief can increase inflammation in our muscles and joints. Deep sadness can cause physical pain. —**Rheumatologist Salome**, who specializes in joints, muscles, and bones

Headaches are one response to grief. —**Neurologist Hassan**

When you are mad or sad, does your stomach hurt? I check to make certain there is no physical problem, like an ulcer, caused by grief. —**Gastroenterologist Mary**, who treats intestinal and stomach problems

Our body's immune system, the protections against disease, can weaken if we grieve for long periods of time. —**Immunologist Hinato,** who researches and treats diseases that involve the immune system

When we experience grief, our bodies may start to show certain symptoms.

- tightness in the chest
- feeling weak
- lack of energy
- nausea
- heart palpitations
- restlessness
- tearfulness

If you are feeling any of the symptoms in the list you just read, go to a Grief Navigator. Find a parent, family member, teacher, faith leader, or counselor. They will be able to give you important guidance. Let the Grief Navigators know that you have learned that these symptoms require professional help.

TRY THIS!

Grief and our emotions affect how our bodies feel. Did you know that it can work the other way around? Engaging in activities like yoga, running, walking, or martial arts increases the neurotransmitter serotonin, which can help improve your mood and energy.

Use the Five-Second Rule. If you find that you are about to do something negative or are about to be overwhelmed by grief, start moving your body for five seconds. Swing your arms! Stomp your feet! Wiggle like a worm! Hop like a bunny! You will be surprised by how five seconds of movement can help.

CHAPTER 4
HOW DOES GRIEF IMPACT YOUR LIFE?

TOP TIP: GRIEF FACTS AND REMINDERS

- Grief is a universal experience. It can happen to anyone. It does happen to everyone.
- Grief affects everything. For a short amount of time, grief changes our bodies and our brains, making it harder to learn, remember, sleep, eat, and pay attention to our relationships.

THE ROLE OF GRIEF IN YOUR LIFE

There are several forms of pain. One type, called acute pain, begins suddenly. It tends to have a sharp quality. Acute pain is a warning that something is threatening your body, mind, and spirit. Grief is one kind of acute pain; it is the kind of pain that accompanies an important loss.

Grief is an important emotion. It is a reminder that you love someone or something that is now gone. Grief is a sign that you have been courageous and vulnerable enough to love someone or something deeply.

Grief makes you human and affects everyone differently. You have learned how grief can change the ways your brain and body work. These changes can have big and small impacts on your life.

School

With the chemicals dancing in your brain, you might experience forgetfulness, confusion, or absent-mindedness. These are all normal responses to grief, but they might make school difficult.

TRY THIS!

- **Keep a journal**. Writing things down will help you remember them for later, and journaling can help you process tough emotions. Try naming three things you learned today. These could be things you learned in class, with a friend, or about yourself.
- **Meditate**. Remember the prefrontal cortex we learned about in the last chapter? Meditation is shown to strengthen our "thinking centers," fighting back against the brain fog that grief can sometimes cause.

Remember that I get larger when you are saddest, and I shrink and disappear as you feel better.

TRY THIS!

Breathing Exercise

- Close your eyes.
- Imagine a small empty balloon in your tummy.
- As you breathe in through your nose, the balloon fills with air and gets bigger.
- As you breathe out through your mouth, the balloon gets smaller and flattens back out.

Relationships

Numbness, loneliness, and irritability might impact the way you interact with those around you. Or you might feel like withdrawing from your friends or avoiding your family. Certain events may feel overwhelming and you'd rather stay home.

TRY THIS!

- **Reach out** to neighbors, family, and friends you trust the most and feel the most comfortable around. If you can, take a deep breath and tell them about what you're feeling.
- **Prepare yourself to experience triggers** of your grief. For example, if Uncle Joe died on Christmas Day, seeing Christmas trees may worsen your grief. Prepare yourself for Christmas by singing Christmas songs, putting up a tree that honors Uncle Joe, making his favorite meal, and talking about your memories.

Hobbies

A lack of energy might prevent you from wanting to participate in sports or other activities. If your grief has grown into depression, you might not enjoy the things that used to bring you joy.

TRY THIS!

- **Make music or art**. Participating in a creative activity requires less physical energy than a sport, so you might find it easier to start. Creating something, whether it's a drawing or a plate of cookies, can give you a big sense of achievement, which will raise your self-esteem.
- **Try positive self-talk**. Think of three things that are great about you. Write them on a sticky note, and place it on a mirror or door where you will see them daily. What are you good at doing? Schedule your phone to remind you to do at least one of those things. For example, it's time to run like the wind around the track! You can also signal your telephone to compliment you. For example, a phone notification can say: "You rocked that solo last concert!" Reminding yourself about what you love to do can inspire you to pick up those activities again.

Health

Grief that feels overwhelming may cause you to stop looking after yourself mentally and physically.

TRY THIS!

Exercise. Exercise releases "feel-good" hormones called endorphins. Walk, swim, cycle, box, or play an organized sport. Yoga is an ancient form of breathing and stretching that relaxes your body and relieves your mind of painful thoughts. It can be a great choice for energizing yourself when you're feeling tired.

TRY THIS!

- **Open Your Heart Pose**. Grief can make your feel closed off. This pose is thought to open your heart. It can help you feel important emotions.
  - Put a small pillow down on the floor.
  - Lie down on your back. Make certain the pillow is in the middle of your back and your head is flat on the floor.
  - Move your legs far apart.
  - Lay your arms on the floor with your hands facing up.
  - Breathe in through your nose and out through your mouth five times.

- **Move Your Body**. After connecting to emotions through the Open Your Heart yoga pose, start moving to get your endorphins going:
  - Stand tall.
  - Move your feet from side to side.
  - Twist your torso from side to side.
  - Swing your arms from side to side.
  - Let your head follow your arms, moving it from side to side.
  - You should now be moving your entire body— your feet, arms, torso, and head. Do you feel like turning the side-to-side movements into a dance? Go right ahead. Have fun!
  - Try to keep your mind free of thoughts. Just enjoy the movement.

Top Tip!

If you're having trouble acting on any of these ideas, talking to a counselor, therapist, or other Grief Navigator might help you take the steps you need toward feeling better.

HOW LONG DOES GRIEF LAST?

Elizabeth Kubler-Ross, a Swiss American psychiatrist, created the "Kubler-Ross Grief Cycle" using a theory about the five stages of grief and loss.

"The reality is that you will grieve forever. You will not 'get over' the loss of a loved one, you will learn to deal with it. You will heal and you will rebuild yourself around the loss you have suffered. You will be whole again, but you will never be the same. Nor should you be the same, nor would you want to."

—Elizabeth Kubler-Ross and John Kessler

Stage One: Denial

Denial means disbelief. When a loss happens, it is normal not to believe it at first. You might talk about a loved one who has died as if they are alive or wait for them to call or text or come to dinner. You might put on your coat and grab your dog's leash for a walk. Denial is a defense mechanism and is a temporary way that we deal with emotions that overwhelm us.

Stage Two: Anger

Pain can sometimes be redirected into anger. Of course you are mad that your family member, friend, or pet has died. Of course you are angry that you just saw another upsetting news story. It's normal to be angry at the person who hurt someone you love or a nice person you learned about on TV or the internet. Even though it may not feel like it, anger is necessary for healing. Anger is an unpleasant, but important, emotion. It can change the way your body feels or cause you to lash out at other people. Anger is a signal that you need to pay attention to your feelings, slow down, and take care of yourself.

TRY THIS!

Create a Scream Box

The anger that you may feel needs someplace to go. It if just rolls around in your brain, it might cause you to lash out at other people. If you push it down into your body, you may have trouble eating, sleeping, and feeling well. Screaming is a great release.

To make a Scream Box you need a cereal box, a paper towel tube, tape, paper, and scissors.

1. Stuff a cereal box with crumpled paper.
2. Close the cereal box and cut a hole in the top for the paper towel tube.
3. Tape the paper towel tube to the hole in the cereal box.
4. Decorate the box however you want.
5. Scream into the box!

49

Stage Three: Bargaining

Bargaining is a stage of grief that allows you to hold on to hope. People sometimes feel guilty about the death of a loved one, the end of a friendship, or their parents' divorce. They might think, "If I had been more obedient, would my parents still be together?" or "If I had taken Fido for a walk, he wouldn't have run out the door and gotten hit by the car. It's all my fault!" People who believe in God might also try to make bargains; they may promise to clean their rooms, do their homework, and obey their parents if God will bring their loved one back to them.

It is easy to ask ourselves, "What if I had done something different?" Do not blame yourself. In the vast majority of cases, your behavior did *not* cause the loss. And even if it contributed somehow, it's important to remember that you cannot change the past. You can only control how you behave in the future.

Stage Four: Depression

A deep sadness settles in as you come to understand that you truly have lost someone or something important. This kind of depression is a natural and appropriate response to grief, not a mental-health condition. Depression may show up as crying, a decreased appetite, changes to how you relate to other people, and problems sleeping. In this stage, you can also feel tired, confused, or unable to enjoy what you once loved doing.

Most importantly, in this stage, you start to face reality about your loss. The depression is the result of realizing that the loss is real, anger will not change the loss, and bargains will not be successful. Acknowledging this is an important and necessary part of your healing journey.

TRY THIS!

Celebrate a Crappy-versary.
You can decide to have a day where you make of list of the reasons you are grieving. It may make you feel sad. After you finish the list, eat something, do a creative activity, write a letter, or have an imaginary conversation with the person who is the reason for your grief.

Stage Five: Acceptance

This is the final stage of grief. You finally know that your loss is real and that it cannot be changed. You may continue to feel sad sometimes, but you are able to function normally.

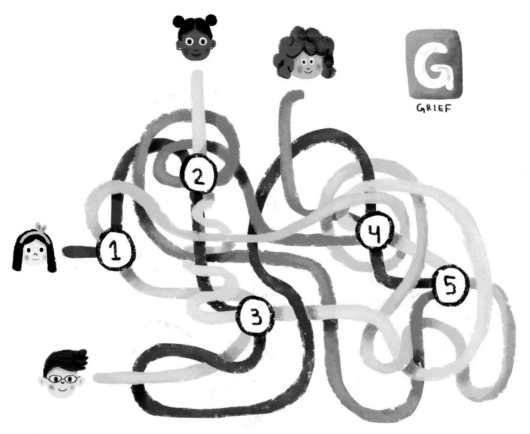

• 1. Denial • 2. Anger • 3. Bargaining • 4. Depression • 5. Acceptance

Remember that there is no one way to grieve. Some kids move through these stages quickly. Some take much longer. Some go through them in order. Others go through them in a different sequence or even repeat an earlier stage. You can go through many intense emotions. It may look to other people as if you have no response at all.

Later in her life, Kubler-Ross changed her five stages of grief. This is called the "Kubler-Ross Change Curve." It has seven overlapping stages instead of five:

1. <u>Shock</u>. Intense and terrible surprise at the loss.
2. <u>Denial</u>. Disbelief and attempts to prove that the loss is not true.
3. <u>Anger and Frustration</u>. Understanding that the loss is real, and anger that it is true.
4. <u>Depression</u>. Intense sadness.
5. <u>Testing</u>. Seeing what the new loss means to your life.
6. <u>Decision</u>. Feeling great about being able to handle the truth about the loss.
7. <u>Integration</u>. Accepting that you had a loss and are fine.

All of these responses are normal.

Different theories are just different ways of understanding your feelings. Exploring these stages of grief and loss can help you understand your own grieving process—or better understand someone else's.

Why are the stages of grief so different for everyone?

The grieving process depends on several factors:

- **Personality** – People have different personalities that may either help them heal quickly from grief or make it harder to heal. Some people get stuck in negative emotions, and some people hide their feelings. Other people get busy; they try to do things rather than talk about how they feel. This is why self-care, talking to other people, and working through some of the strategies noted by the Grief Navigators are important.

- **Age** – Life experiences, especially previous experiences with grief, can make new grief easier to manage. For this reason, sometimes adults move through the stages of grief more quickly than children do.

- **Beliefs** – Our beliefs affect how we move through the stages of grief. For example, sometimes people believe that their sadness honors the loss or grief they have experienced. It does not. The person you lost made you happy; they would not want you to be sad because they are gone. Remember the good times and smile. It is fine to be sad for a while, but you only hurt yourself by holding onto pain.

- **Support Network** – If you have friends, family, and adults at home who you can speak to about your feelings, you might heal faster than kids who cannot identify a helpful person. Luckily, there are now online support networks that can help.

- **The Type of Loss** – We have learned about different kinds of grief and loss. Major sources of grief are most often associated with death, natural disasters, and changing homes or schools. The more significant a loss is to you, the more intense the grief may be.

Loss can make it seem as if the whole world has changed. Some will adapt and adjust quickly to the changes in their lives. They may feel better in a few weeks or months. Others will experience grief that lasts a longer time, from months to years.

Some research shows us that grief lasts from six months to four years. The worst symptoms of grief—depression, sleeplessness, loss of appetite—tend to begin resolving at six months.

The important thing to remember is that you will heal if you understand your emotions; take care of yourself by exercising, sleeping, and eating well; and get professional help. The sooner you start to address your feelings and fears, the faster you are likely to feel better.

WHAT IS THE BEST WAY TO GRIEVE?

There is no wrong way to grieve, unless you are harming yourself or others. Here are some misconceptions about grieving:

I am doing it wrong.

I should be feeling . . .

I am not going through the stages of grief in the right way.

Remember: The Kubler-Ross Grief Cycle is an idea that helps many people understand their grief, but it isn't an exact guide to grief. You can experience one stage for a long time. You might not really experience all stages, or you might repeat a stage. How you experience your grief is unique to YOU.

Is it OK to still have fun?

It is possible to feel grief and happiness at the same time. Your grief is about a specific person or experience or event. The rest of your life can be filled with happiness and joy. You can be silly and goofy. Having fun is a great way to honor the life of your loved one who has died or gone away. People who love you don't want you to be miserable. They want you to have a fabulous life, even when they are no longer part of it.

CHAPTER 5
TAKING CONTROL OF YOUR GRIEF

WILL YOU EVER BE OK AGAIN?

Yes, you will be OK again. Feeling better is a process that starts with your wish to feel better, your decision to use available resources, and patience. Healing takes time. Healing is also a decision that requires your hard work. You are reading this book, and that is a great start!

HOW SHOULD YOU MANAGE YOUR GRIEF?

Just as grief is a very personal experience, recovery is different for everyone. There is not just one way to recover from grief. However, there are many great recovery strategies.

Allow yourself to grieve.

It is painful to accept that you have lost someone or something special to you. Take time to understand your grief by rereading sections of this book, talking to a Grief Navigator, or keeping a journal.

HEALING CHART

PROGRESS

TIME

TRY THIS!

Keep a journal (or two). You can use any notebook for this. Write down your thoughts, emotions, fears, and concerns. You can draw pictures or write poetry, songs, or stories about the person you lost or about an experience that is making you deeply sad.

Finish the sentence

In your Grief Journal, finish the following sentences:
The thing that makes me feel the saddest is . . .
If I could talk to the person who died, I would ask/say . . .

Since the death of _____, my family doesn't . . .
My worst memory is . . .
If I could change things, I would . . .
One thing I liked to do with the person who died was . . .
When the person died, I . . .
Since the death, my friends . . .
After the death, school . . .
When I am alone . . .

Make the decision to heal.

Getting better takes work and requires making the decision to put in the effort. Remember that this takes time, tears, and talking about your feelings. Sad feelings tend to go away over time. Deep sadness takes longer. If you feel like your sadness isn't fading, it might help to talk with a Grief Navigator. With their help, you can learn to manage your emotions. You can decide it is time to put your grief behind you and to grasp a happier future.

Look to the future.

When handling one day at a time starts to feel manageable, making future plans is an excellent way to help you feel better. Human beings crave the feeling of being in control of themselves and their environments. Scientists believe that having a plan for the future is a great way to relieve emotional stress and to create the patterns that allow us to have control over our behaviors.

Reduce anxiety.

Practices like meditation and deep breathing help make you mindful of how you are feeling and what your body is doing. These exercises help you become aware of your thoughts, feelings, body, and surroundings. Meditation helps you accept what you think and feel without any negative judgments. Deep breathing calms your body when you are anxious. It helps get rid of Grief Brain and allows you to focus on your thoughts. From this practice, positive thoughts can grow. It is hard to grieve when you are practicing positive thinking.

Here is an exercise that mixes breathing and meditation. Your lungs will expand and contract. You will visualize your grief. This exercise involves imagining me!

TRY THIS!

Breathing Exercise

- Sit in a straight chair or lie down on a flat surface (floor or bed).
- Relax your shoulders.
- Close your eyes.
- Breathe in and out normally.
- When you are ready, breathe in through your nose. Imagine bricks becoming a wall in front of you.
- The next time you exhale, breathe out slowly from your mouth. Imagine the brick wall coming down, brick by brick.
- Take five breaths. Five breaths = five walls being built brick by brick and five walls coming down brick by brick.

Create positive memories.

Creating memories, especially happy ones, is essential to your mental health.

Happy memories help you strengthen your sense of personal identity and purpose in life.

Happy memories help you make relationship bonds that bring you close to your family and friends.

Happiness strengthens your relationship to the earth and everyone on it.

Here is a math equation about creating happy memories:
Picking good memories from the PAST +
Planning for the FUTURE = Happiness NOW!

TRY THIS!

Create a Memory Book

This is a special kind of scrapbook that supports emotional wellness after you have experienced a loss. To make a Memory Book, you can use colored paper, crayons, pens or markers, paper fasteners, yarn, string, staples, tape, glitter glue, and stickers.

1. Using your materials, draw your favorite memories of the person, pet, or experience that is causing you to feel grief.
2. Write captions to go along with these pictures.
3. Stack the pages together and place a blank sheet of paper on top. This will be the cover to your Memory Book. Then, either staple or punch holes near one edge of the paper. If you punch holes, tie with string or yarn, or secure with paper fasteners.
4. Decorate the cover of your Memory Book with anything you'd like: stickers, glitter, more pictures, etc. What will the title of your Memory Book be?

If you have other items that remind you of the person, pet, or experience, you can place these (and your Memory Book) in a Memory Box. This can be any box that you decorate—a designated place to keep things like letters, photos, and meaningful objects.

Remember special days.

Birthdays, anniversaries, and holidays can be hard when we have suffered loss. But finding ways to remember your loved one on these days is important. You must learn to remember the wonderful moments of their life, rather than focusing on their death.

Gather paper, colored pens and pencils, scissors, glue, glitter, and other special elements that remind you of your loved one. For example, maybe your loved one always baked something special for holidays. If you are making a collage, you could include a photo of that food, a wrapper, or a box label. Or you could draw a memory you have of them making and enjoying their favorite food.

TRY THIS!

Memory in Action

Here are some examples of memory in action, using the behaviors and habits of the person you are grieving:

- What was your loved one's favorite food? Eat it on their birthday.
- What was your loved one's favorite sports team? Watch a game and mimic how your loved one responded to wins and losses. Eat their favorite snacks.
- Wear your loved one's favorite color on their birthday.

You will think of other examples. The important point is to create new memories from the old memories.

Take care of your health

Grief disrupts your regular patterns of sleeping and eating. Try to exercise, especially when you don't want to. Set reminders to eat healthy meals. Go to bed at your regular time. Keeping your body healthy may shorten your grieving period.

Creating memories, especially happy ones, is essential to your mental health.

What forms of exercise are useful ways to combat grief? Almost any! Even though these activities are probably the last thing you want to do, try! Afterward, because of how your brain chemistry works when you move your body, you will begin to feel better. Here are some ideas:

- Walk or ride your bike in your neighborhood or local park. Walk alone, with family or friends, or with a pet. Take in your surroundings. What do you see on your walk? Hear? Smell?
- If there is not a safe place to walk or bike in your neighborhood, march around your house.
- Dance. We have already discussed how endorphins flood our brains and bodies when we move our bodies freely. We have discussed how important it is for human beings to feel as if they have some control over their lives. Dance heals because it mixes emotional control with physical movement. For these reasons, dance is a perfect tool for healing. Play music through a speaker or put on headphones and dance. If you belong to a group that has experienced a loss, try choreographing a dance together. You can let your body talk and forget, for a moment, without using your words.
- And don't forget the Five-Second Rule!

Be patient with yourself.

You may not feel like playing your musical instrument or engaging in sports like baseball or soccer right now. That's fine. You'll get back to these activities. Start with what feels manageable to you right now, and reach out if you need help making the next step. Remember, everyone grieves at their own pace.

Talk to someone.

Grief is hard to get through without help. Talking to members of your family, to teachers, and to other responsible adults, especially those who have shared your experience, can be helpful.

A professionally trained therapist is also useful in many ways.

Therapists can help you

- discuss your feelings in a neutral and safe space.
- develop a healthy outlook on death, trauma, and loss.
- understand what you are feeling.
- learn coping skills to manage your grief, depression, and anger.
- provide strategies to return to your normal routine.

TRY THIS!

Write a Letter

If talking to someone in person feels overwhelming at first, try writing a letter that explains in detail the events and feelings you'd like to share.

WHEN SHOULD YOU REACH OUT TO A TRAINED PROFESSIONAL?

The best strategy is to immediately connect with the Grief Navigators available to you. This way, you can ward off problems that may develop if you try to manage everything on your own. If you don't make an immediate connection with a navigator, and your grief has not improved in four to six weeks, it is very important that you get help from a trained counselor, therapist, psychologist, medical doctor, or psychiatrist. There may be other people, like a faith leader or teacher, with training that can be helpful. Let a trusted adult know you need help as soon as possible. Be clear how important their assistance is to your well-being.

You should talk to a professional if you have any of the following experiences:

- Feelings of deep sadness, depression, and hopelessness.
- Problems managing your normal routine, like going to school, playing sports, doing your homework and chores, sleeping, eating, and getting along with other people.
- Blaming yourself and believing that the loss is your fault.
- Wanting to hurt yourself or someone else.
- Thoughts that your life is no longer worth living.

You can also use a combination of professional resources. For example, you can talk to a faith leader about your religious or spiritual questions and concerns, and talk to a psychologist about sadness, anger, and problems sleeping and eating. If sadness has turned to depression, you may require medication for a while. Prescriptions can be written by medical doctors. Your family doctor or a psychiatrist will be helpful in determining if you can benefit from medication and, if so, what medicine is most likely to help you.

We've explored several ways to imagine grief, such as Brickmason BOW and Tilly Tumbleweed. Another metaphor for grief is the invisible suitcase. Traumatic events cause us to lug around our pain like it is a heavy suitcase. You take it to school, community events, and family functions. This suitcase holds your feelings and memories. When you don't manage your emotions, the invisible suitcase gets big. It opens up and spills things out when you don't want it to. When this happens, don't hesitate to get help with managing your grief.

WHAT ARE SOME OTHER WAYS TO MANAGE GRIEF?

You can engage in other grief-managing strategies alongside therapy. We've already covered a few. Here are some more:

Make or listen to music.

Sing songs, listen to music, or play music. Music is a very powerful healing tool during times of loss. Songs remind us of the person we love and have lost. They remind us of the traumatic event. Because grief can unleash powerful and sometimes scary emotions, music gives us safe access to our deepest feelings. Music gives us space to grieve when we may not have the words to describe how we feel. Especially when we grieve in community, music allows us to connect with others who are also grieving.

Try a writing exercise.

Write a letter to the loved one you lost to death or who is suffering a difficult illness. Write in your Grief Journal about an event or experience that caused you to grieve. Write a poem about the person or pet about whom you are grieving or focused on the event that caused you grief.

These exercises can be included in your Memory Box or Memory Book. Be certain to show what you have written to your counselor. It will be a great way to start a conversation about your feelings.

Meditate.

Deep breathing and learning to focus on your breath help many distractions in your life disappear, even if for a short time. We've practiced a couple deep-breathing exercises already. You can repeat these or find ideas through meditation apps and videos that help kids cope with grief and loss.

Try aromatherapy.

Aromatherapy can help relieve stress, and grief is a form of stress. Essential oils cannot cure grief, but they may help you manage negative emotions and the physical effects of grief.

TRY THIS!

Essential Oils Can Help You Manage Your Grief

Put a couple of drops in your body lotion or coconut oil to spread them smoothly on your body. Take a look at the chart to the right for help on deciding which essential oil might be right for you. Ask an adult for help using each of these.

ESSENTIAL OIL	HELPS REDUCE	HELPS INCREASE/ IMPROVE	HOW TO USE
Lavender	Anger Anxiety Depression Symptoms from post-traumatic stress disorder (PTSD)	Calm Comfort	Rub on wrists Spray on pillow
Jasmine	Worries	Energy Focus	Inhale
Frankincense	Inflammation in the body Bacteria in the body Fungus in the body	Health Peace of mind Harmony Digestion Physical pain Immunity	Rub on wrists Inhale
Sandalwood	Irritation Trouble sleeping	Sleep Mood Relaxation	Rub on wrists Inhale
Chamomile	Anger Anxiety Irritation	Emotional balance Peace of mind	Rub on wrists Inhale
Mandarin	Stress Nervousness Pain Anxiety Nausea	Sleep Relaxation Calm	Rub on wrists Inhale Spray on pillow

HOW TO HELP SOMEONE WHO'S GRIEVING

Most of this chapter has focused on how to manage your own grief. Perhaps you are not directly impacted by a loss but have a friend who is. What do you do?

Know the basics.

- Understand what grief is.
- Understand the grieving process.

Know the do's and don'ts for conversations about grief.

DO:

- Contact them to check in.
- Listen more than you talk.
- Ask questions to understand their experience and feelings.
- Acknowledge your friend's grief.
- Be willing and able to sit in silence.

DON'T:

- Don't be afraid to talk to your friend about their loss.
- Don't try to fix your friend or family member.
- Don't talk about your own grief.
- Don't talk about the appearance of the person who is grieving.
- Don't talk about God or religion unless they bring up the topic.

Be practical.

- Give your grieving friend or relative a "Month of Mondays." On Mondays, run errands for them. Bring them their homework if they have missed class, pick up a library book, or walk their dog.
- Do chores for others. You can be helpful by doing chores that the grieving person can't do right now. If a parent or guardian is grieving, help out more around the house. If your next-door neighbor loses their partner, you can sweep their sidewalks clean, pull weeds from their flowerbeds, or rake the leaves in their yard. (Before helping out, make sure you get permission!)

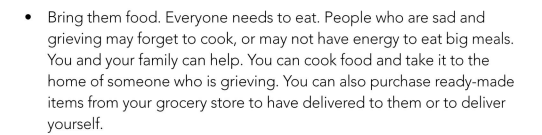

- Bring them food. Everyone needs to eat. People who are sad and grieving may forget to cook, or may not have energy to eat big meals. You and your family can help. You can cook food and take it to the home of someone who is grieving. You can also purchase ready-made items from your grocery store to have delivered to them or to deliver yourself.

Be sure to find out if the friends or family you are feeding have food allergies or special dietary needs. Learning this information allows you to plan the healthiest meals for them. A quick online search will provide you with recipes that fit most dietary needs.

Send your support.

Text your support (but don't expect a response). You can send a short text for a few days to remind the person you're there for them:

- I am thinking about you.
- You are not alone.
- Your feelings are important.
- I am here to support you in the ways that you need.

Remember important dates.

Make a note of special dates, like birthdays, death days, and anniversaries. On those days, do something special for your friend or relative. Bake their loved one's favorite cake or send a card through the mail.

Share your grief strategies

For example, if art has helped you, try drawing, coloring, or painting with the grieving person, if they want.

When you visit your friend or family member, you can bring paper and art materials. Put them in the middle of the table. You can say, "I'm going to make a drawing of how I remember (insert person's name)." Don't ask them to draw or paint with you. Then sit quietly and draw. If your friend or relative wants to join this activity, they will.

Include your friend on walks or other activities you enjoy together. Present the opportunity and let them decide whether they'd like to join.

CONCLUSION
YOU'VE GOT THIS

Remember that grief is a common human emotion. Your memories won't be painful forever. Grieving means that you are capable of loving someone or something. You have a big heart that loves deeply. Grief is not fun, but you've got this!

Most importantly, you have the tools to manage your grief.

- **Pay attention** to how much your grief weighs. Check the size of Tilly Tumbleweed and the height of Brickmason BOW.

- **Release fear**. Remember that you are experiencing something normal, and go with it.

- **Stay healthy** by eating well, exercising regularly, and getting sleep that refreshes you.

- **Use your talents** and skills to feel better. (See the exercises in Chapter Five.)

- **Embody strength**. Your body sometimes holds sadness. It also holds lots of strength.
- **Be patient with yourself**. Recovering from grief takes time.
- **Check in with your Grief Navigators**. Identify someone who knows how to listen when you want to talk. Your Grief Navigator can be someone your own age, a sibling, relative, parent, caregiver, or therapist.

Does grief ever go away?

This is a complicated question. If you are wondering if you will ever stop grieving, the short answer is no. Grief stays with us because the love we feel for the person who died never goes away. You may also be reminded of experiences that caused you grief but that might not involve death.

Healing from grief is the most important goal. You heal when you learn how to manage your grief. The loss that you experienced gets integrated into your daily life. Your experience of loss changes how you interact with other people and how you experience the world.

Here are some examples of how people have integrated grief into their lives:

- One grandfather loved cinnamon rolls, so on his birthday, his family had cinnamon rolls for breakfast and told stories about Grandpa.
- An uncle died who had been a Tuskegee Airman, a member of a group of African American pilots who fought in World War II. When this man died, his niece wrote an article about him, located photos of him, and found an American flag. To honor her uncle's life, she put these items in a chair during the family's Thanksgiving dinner. Each person in the family discussed what he had meant to them.
- The family dog was hit by a car. On his birthday, the family sat on a hill in their back yard and looked at funny videos of their pet.

In all of these examples, individuals and families were able to hold their grief, joy, and memories in the same bucket of feelings. They talked about their love for the person or pet they had lost. They were fine. You will be too.

Sigmund Freud is considered the "father of psychology." Dr. Freud said that after you experience loss, you will mourn and be sad for a time. He believed that it was healthy that we can never replace the person, thing, or experience that causes us to grieve. Freud believed that, once you have healed from grief, your daily life should leave a space in which whoever or whatever you lost can stay. You can have an annual ceremony for a loved one. You can miss your grandmother and smile. You can make the cake that you helped Grandma bake and not be sad. You can smell her perfume and recall how wonderful it was to breathe in that aroma when she hugged you. There may still be a pang of loss in your heart because she is gone, but there can also be joy.

You will know that you are healed when joy and grief occur at the same time but you can manage your emotions, enjoy your memories, and keep moving forward.

Healing = Joy + Grief + Memories + Deciding to Move Toward the Future

YOU ARE NEVER ALONE (ADDITIONAL RESOURCES)

If you're not sure where to start, the following are all places you or a Grief Navigator can look for good advice about healing from grief. No matter which steps you take, remember that you never need to deal with this alone.

- **Dougy Center**: The Dougy Center provides support and resources for talking to children who are grieving a death. It is part of the National Center for Grieving Children and Families. There is also useful information about talking with kids about school shootings and other mass tragedies. www.dougy.org
- **Teenage Grief Sucks**: A teen-run site filled with real stories from other kids like you. Hearing from others may help you feel less alone. www.teenagegriefsucks.com
- **What's Your Grief?**: Whether you're grieving or helping out someone else, this site explores ideas, experiences, and concepts through courses, books, helpful blog posts, and more. https://whatsyourgrief.com
- **The National Alliance for Children's Grief (NACG)**: The NACG website provides toolkits, resources, and help finding support for grieving kids. www.childrengrieve.org

Webexplorer

grief help

www.dougy.org
www.teenagegriefsucks.com
www.whatsyourgrief.com
www.childrengrieve.org

Dr. Lora-Ellen McKinney is a psychologist who has worked with, researched, and taught about children, families, and supportive or harmful systems. She worked in public health policy, conducting research and writing legislation. Dr. McKinney graduated from Vassar College, the University of Washington, and the Harvard Kennedy School.

Greek-born and Athens-based **Sophia Touliatou** has studied graphic design and works as an illustrator, doing mostly children books, many of which have gained merits and awards.